HOLIDAY HOUSE
NEW YORK

ST. PATRICK'S DAY

BY GAIL GIBBONS

To Barbara Walsh

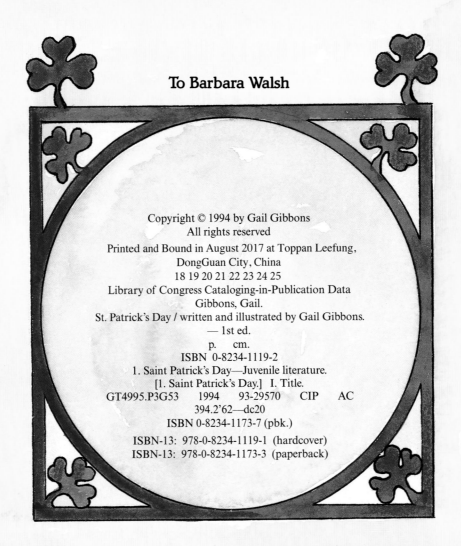

Copyright © 1994 by Gail Gibbons
All rights reserved
Printed and Bound in August 2017 at Toppan Leefung,
DongGuan City, China
18 19 20 21 22 23 24 25
Library of Congress Cataloging-in-Publication Data
Gibbons, Gail.
St. Patrick's Day / written and illustrated by Gail Gibbons.
— 1st ed.
p.   cm.
ISBN 0-8234-1119-2
1. Saint Patrick's Day—Juvenile literature.
[1. Saint Patrick's Day.]   I. Title.
GT4995.P3G53   1994   93-29570   CIP   AC
394.2'62—dc20
ISBN 0-8234-1173-7 (pbk.)

ISBN-13: 978-0-8234-1119-1 (hardcover)
ISBN-13: 978-0-8234-1173-3 (paperback)

St. Patrick's Day is celebrated each year on March 17th.

This holiday is celebrated by the Irish and other people in many parts of the world. They honor Saint Patrick, the patron saint of Ireland.

Saint Patrick lived many years ago. He was born in Britain around the year 380 and raised in a Christian family. His parents didn't name him Patrick. Some people believe his name was Maewyn.

While still a boy he was kidnapped and brought to Ireland where he was made a slave. His captors forced him to herd sheep. He prayed that God would help him. Six years later he escaped.

After finally arriving back in Britain, he lived quietly, thought, and prayed. He realized what he wanted to do. He had dreams of returning to Ireland to teach the people about God.

He went to France to study religion. In the year 432, the head of the Catholic Church, the Pope, named him Patricius, the Latin name for Patrick. He became a priest and then a bishop.

At last, Bishop Patrick's dreams came true. He sailed back
to Ireland and began preaching. He built churches and
schools all over the country. People noticed his kind ways
and trusted him.

Bishop Patrick spent the rest of his life caring for the Irish people. They loved this kind man.

People honor Patrick on March 17th because he died on that date in the year 461. Later, the Catholic Church made him a saint . . . Saint Patrick.

Today, many things are done to celebrate this holiday. People go to church to give thanks to Saint Patrick for his work in Ireland.

People have fun, too. They dress in green to honor an ancient Irish custom. Hundreds of years ago the people of Ireland burned branches with green leaves during the month of March and spread the ashes in fields to make them fertile and green. To wear green is to honor Ireland, the Emerald Isle.

Decorations are put on doors and windows. Shamrocks appear everywhere. The shamrock is a plant that has three leaves and looks like clover. It is the symbol of Saint Patrick as well as of Ireland.

Leprechauns are remembered on St. Patrick's Day. Long ago, some Irish folk believed in these little magic creatures. It was thought if you caught a leprechaun, you could make him lead you to a pot of gold. Leprechaun comes from the Old Irish word *Luchorpan*, meaning wee one. People believed they were only as big as your thumb.

There is the shillelagh, too. In Ireland, many years ago,
there was an old oak forest called Shillelagh. The Irish liked
to own a "sprig of shillelagh," a short oak club from the forest. Often, people decorate shillelaghs with green ribbons.

The harp is one of the oldest musical instruments and has been popular with the Irish people since early times. It serves as another St. Patrick's Day decoration.

On St. Patrick's Day people may give cards to their families and friends.

People also make cakes, cookies and goodies to share with others.

Some people give flowers. Others wear green carnations or pin shamrocks to their clothes to celebrate the holiday.

There may be St. Patrick's Day plays, too.

Some families and friends have quiet times together in re-
membrance of Saint Patrick. Often there are meals to share.

St. Patrick's Day parties are given, too. It is fun to sing Irish songs, dance Irish jigs and play games.

In many places there are St. Patrick's Day parades. Flags flutter in the wind. Pipers and fiddlers play Irish tunes.

There are green hats, people in costumes, green banners
. . . lots of green!

The first time St. Patrick's Day was celebrated in the
United States was in 1737 in Boston. Each year the Irish
and many other people love to celebrate St. Patrick's Day.

For many people it is a day for worship and for celebration,
and if you're not Irish, to feel a little bit Irish!

Saint Patrick and the Snakes

It is said that Saint Patrick got rid of all the snakes in Ireland. By beating his drum, he frightened them into the sea. Today there are no snakes in Ireland.

Saint Patrick and the Poison

Some people say that a wizard tried to kill Saint Patrick by putting poison in his drink. Saint Patrick quickly turned it into ice and tossed it from his cup.

Saint Patrick and His Cloak

It is said that Saint Patrick had a friend who borrowed his cloak. There was a big fire where the friend was staying, but he was not hurt because he was wearing Saint Patrick's cloak.

Saint Patrick and the Shamrock

Saint Patrick used the shamrock to explain to people about the Holy Trinity, one God in three divine beings, the Father, the Son and the Holy Spirit. Growing at his feet was a shamrock. He used this plant to explain three in one, one stem with three leaves.

Saint Patrick and the Fish

Another legend is that each year on March 17th, fish rise from the sea. They pass before St. Patrick's altar in Ireland and then disappear back into the sea.

Saint Patrick and the Sunset

It is said that the sun didn't set when Saint Patrick died and that it shone in the sky for twelve days and nights.